the **WRITER** says

Also available in the
Words of Wisdom series:

The Architect Says
Laura S. Dushkes

The Designer Says
Sara Bader

The Filmmaker Says
Jamie Thompson Stern

The Chef Says
Nach Waxman and Matt Sartwell

The Musician Says
Benedetta LoBalbo

The Inventor Says
Kevin Lippert

the
WRITER
says

*Quotes, Quips,
and Words
of Wisdom*

compiled & edited by Kevin Lippert

Princeton Architectural Press, New York

This is the seventh volume in our informally named Words of Wisdom series, which includes collections of quotes and quips from architects, designers, musicians, filmmakers, chefs, and inventors. Typically, these are library research projects (the series was inspired by librarian Laura Dushke's collection of quotes from architects, which became *The Architect Says*). The process involves finding, verifying, and organizing quotes, a sometimes painstaking effort. This book, however, was more akin to filling a Dixie cup from a fire hose, so large is the universe of advice to and from writers, in the form of books, articles, interviews, websites, and courses. Writers don't agree about what to write about, or how, but do seem to agree there's always room for one more book on the shelf of writing advice.

The quotes come from many different kinds of writers, including novelists, personal essayists, grammarians, academics, and journalists, but certain threads are common: the necessity of a good work space, a diligent work schedule, and perseverance (Annie Lamott's oft-quoted dictum "Butt in chair," from her wise and funny *Bird by Bird*, is repeated in many iterations), the need for a good editor (I've been extremely fortunate to have one of the best in the business, Sara Stemen, as mine), and the absolute necessity of reading in general—widely, often, and carefully. Whether or not you're a writer and use this book for inspiration, fun, or not at all, this exhortation to read is music to a publisher's ears, and I'm delighted you've made room in your reading and writing schedule for this slim volume. I hope you find some nuggets to invigorate and amuse, as I did.

While this is by no means a how-to book, it draws from much of the landscape of books about writing, from the ups and downs of the writing life (as in Dani Shapiro's heartfelt and honest *Still Writing*) to discussions of what makes fiction effective (E. M. Forster's witty *Aspects of the Novel*) to the mechanics and poetics of wordsmithing (Verlyn Klinkenborg's *Several Short Sentences about Writing* and Richard Goodman's *The Soul of Creative Writing*). Indeed, anyone interested in writing and the power of language will be richer for diving into any of the sources here.

Kevin Lippert
Hudson, New York
November 2017

WRITING IS AN ACT OF COURAGE.

Ta-Nehisi Coates (1975–)

What writing is: telepathy, of course.

Stephen King (1947–)

The great power of literature… is that if 1,000 people read the same book, the book reads each of them differently.

David Grossman (1954–)

Words, English words, are
full of echoes, of memories,
of associations. They have been
out and about, on people's lips,
in their houses, in the streets,
in the fields, for so many
centuries. And that is one of
the chief difficulties in writing
them today—that they are
stored with other meanings,
with other memories, and they
have contracted so many
famous marriages in the past.

Virginia Woolf (1882–1941)

Beware of a writer quoting too much; he may be quoting all he knows.

Alfred Kazin (1915–98)

YOU CAN ONLY BECOME A BETTER WRITER BY BECOMING A BETTER READER.

Verlyn Klinkenborg (1952–)

What I wrote when I was very young had some of the characteristic qualities of every writer I had any feeling for. It takes a while before that admiration sinks back and becomes unconscious. The writers stay with you for the rest of your life. But at least they don't intrude and become visible to the reader.

William Maxwell (1908–2000)

My childhood was aberrant and peculiar and nomadic and absolutely unpredictable....The mixture of solitude and uncertainty fertilized the situation enormously.... Inevitably I was making up stories to myself, retreating into myself.

John le Carré (1931–)

Writing for me is to a large extent self-entertainment, and the only child is driven to do that. For example, I'm an expert whistler…but that takes hours of practice, the sort of thing one hasn't got time for if one's part of a large family, I imagine.

Kingsley Amis (1922–95)

When I was between fourteen and eighteen I was a delinquent teenager, always in trouble, breaking the law, doing drugs. Then I became a successful writer, and it has sort of worked out.

Hanif Kureishi (1954–)

IF I HADN'T WRITTEN, I PROBABLY WOULD HAVE DONE SOMETHING STUPID THAT WOULD HAVE LED TO MY DEATH.

Octavia Butler (1947–2006)

Some kids liked to play tennis, I liked to write. I wasn't out hanging out or doing a lot of stuff teens were doing, because what I liked to do was be in my room and type.

S. E. Hinton (1948–)

I… looked back to myself as a sixteen-year-old and how much I loved reading and how a book could completely change my life…so I just like the idea of trying to write for all those versions of me out there, wherever they are.

Sherman Alexie (1966–)

I STARTED WRITING MY OWN THINGS WHEN I WAS TWELVE, THIRTEEN, AND I KNOW WHY I DID IT—MAINLY BECAUSE I HAD FINISHED ALL THE ADVENTURE NOVELS, MUSKETEER NOVELS, AND DUMAS THAT I WAS READING AT THE TIME. THEN I FOUND OUT I COULD WRITE THEM MYSELF.

Javier Marías (1951–)

Finally, after all these years of reading books, editing books, working in libraries, I thought, "Wait a minute, there's no book in there about me!" So if I wanted to read it, I would probably have to write it.

Toni Morrison (1931–)

My family has been the biggest thing in my life. It is much more than just a resource for my writing. I have always felt like the son in some ways. I think that's true of all extended families, as true of Italian or Jewish families as Indian ones. You never gain independence. In your imagination, you are always someone's child, long dead though they may be.

Vikram Seth (1952–)

Your mother will not make you a writer. My advice to any young person who wants to write is: leave home.

Paul Theroux (1941–)

I decided to become a writer. It was a good idea. Having had no experience whatever in writing, except writing letters and reports, I wasn't handicapped by exaggerated notions of the difficulties ahead.

Dashiell Hammett (1894–1961)

I JUST KNEW I WOULD BE A WRITER. IT JUST SEEMED THE ONLY SENSIBLE THING TO DO.

Jane Gardam (1928–)

If you get right out of college and expect (or want) to get a job as a writer, you might be making a mistake. You might be better off working on a merchant ship or a cannery or a hospital—something new, something where you might learn a thing or two.

Dave Eggers (1970–)

Do something else. Because what's going to happen in the next five years if you stay within your niche is already so circumscribed and predictable. And what can happen if you leave it and do something else is unknown, and therefore bigger. Experiences like these, and the people you'll meet, can inform your work in the future in so many ways.

Chris Kraus (1955–)

You can teach people a lot about craft and various techniques, and you can certainly teach them to appreciate, but you *cannot* give them spirit or soul if it's not there.

Mary Gaitskill (1954–)

Understand that everyone has 1,000 pages of bad fiction in him or her, and before you can do anything, you probably have to just write your thousand pages of crap.

Jennifer Finney Boylan (1958–)

THE FIRST THING A WRITER HAS TO DO IS FIND ANOTHER SOURCE OF INCOME.

Ellen Gilchrist (1935–)

I FEEL THAT I HAVE NOT TALENTS
WHATSOEVER IN MONEY AND
BUSINESS MATTERS. SO MAYBE
I OUGHT NOT TO DO WITH IT AT ALL.
I GET TOO THOROUGHLY IMMERSED
IN MY DREAMS. BUT SOMEHOW
LIFE IS SO ORGANIZED THAT I FIND
MYSELF TIED TO MONEY MATTERS
LIKE A GRAZING HORSE TO A STAKE.

Zora Neale Hurston (1891–1960)

I don't think I've ever felt, before or since, anything like the elation of realizing I was going to be published.

J. K. Rowling (1965–)

I really felt I peaked when I saw my first novel in print.

Herman Koch (1953–)

I like Hollywood.…
Honestly, if I were a
generation younger,
I probably would
have started with
TV instead of books.

Gary Shteyngart (1972–)

Let me not imply that there are no writers of authentic ability in Hollywood. There are not many, but there are not many anywhere.

Raymond Chandler (1888–1959)

I THINK OF MYSELF AS
A NEW YORK WRITER
EVEN WHEN I AM NOT
IN NEW YORK, AND BY
THAT I MEAN, I THINK
THE VALUES AND
THEMES OF NEW YORK—
UNIQUENESS, AMBITION,
OUTSIDERS/INSIDERS,
FAILURE, GRANDIOSITY,
AND HUMILIATION—
ARE DEEPLY INGRAINED
IN MY POINT OF VIEW.

Min Jin Lee (1968–)

AS A NATIVE NEW YORKER, REAL ESTATE IS ALWAYS, ALWAYS INTERESTING TO ME.

Emma Straub (1980–)

The longer I work at the craft of writing, the more I realize that there's nothing more interesting than the truth.... Who could invent all the astonishing things that really happen? I increasingly find myself saying to writers and students, "Trust your material."

William Zinsser (1922–2015)

I love the details of
a novel. For research,
I like to go to the
location of the places
in the novels. The first
thing that I do is involve
my senses: I notice
the smells; I open the
trash cans and look
at what people have
thrown away.

Natsuo Kirino (1951–)

I don't think I've ever written about a part of the world which I myself haven't visited. But you see, I was a reporter for a long time. I have a reporter's eye and sense of locality, and I add to this by taking notes and buying road maps wherever I happen to be.

Ian Fleming (1908–64)

WE'VE ALL READ NOVELS
WHERE YOU PLOW THROUGH
THREE PAGES ON THE
MANUFACTURE OF RUBBER
AND YOU REALIZE THAT
THE WRITER HAS BEEN
TO SINGAPORE TO SEE
A RUBBER PLANTATION
AND BY GOD ARE WE GOING
TO HEAR ABOUT IT.

William Boyd (1952–)

If you want to find a magical situation, magical things, you have to go deep inside yourself. So that is what I do. People say it's magic realism— but in the depths of my soul, it's just realism. Not magical. While I'm writing, it's very natural, very logical, very realistic and reasonable.

Haruki Murakami (1949–)

There's not a line
in any of my books
which I can't connect
to a real experience.
There is always
a reference to a
concrete reality.

Gabriel García Márquez (1927–2014)

ONE WRITES OUT OF ONE THING ONLY—ONE'S OWN EXPERIENCE. EVERYTHING DEPENDS ON HOW RELENTLESSLY ONE FORCES FROM THIS EXPERIENCE THE LAST DROP, SWEET OR BITTER, IT CAN POSSIBLY GIVE.

James Baldwin (1924–87)

CROSSING BORDERS MEANS
THAT AT TIMES *I SHARE THINGS
THAT I DON'T WANT TO SHARE.*
BUT IF YOU REALLY SEE YOURSELF
AS A WORKER FOR FREEDOM,
THEN THE CHALLENGE IS ALSO
ON YOU TO SACRIFICE WHATEVER
NOTIONS OF PRIVACY THAT
MANY OF US WOULD WANT
TO HOLD ON TO.

bell hooks (1952–)

I really want to escape myself as much as I can—myself as the artist, or as the writer, or as the thinker.

Chang-Rae Lee (1965–)

The best way for me to solve problems in my own life is to write about them.

Peter Straub (1943–)

I don't write for my friends or myself, either; I write for *it*, for the pleasure of *it*. I believe if I stopped to wonder what so-and-so would think, or what I'd feel like if this were read by a stranger, I would be paralyzed.

Eudora Welty (1909–2001)

DON'T WRITE TO TRENDS, AND LET THE MARKETPLACE COME TO YOU.

Jeff VanderMeer (1968–)

Historically, the books that have persevered in our culture and in our memories and our hearts were not the literary fiction of the day but the popular fiction of the day.

Jodi Picoult (1966–)

You don't have to burn books to destroy a culture. Just get people to stop reading them.

Ray Bradbury (1920–2012)

There are few things that depress me more than hearing the word "great" followed by a nationality and then the word "novel." There is no such thing as the great anything novel.

Marlon James (1970–)

THERE'S NO
GREAT LITERARY
TRADITION.
THERE'S ONLY
THE TRADITION
OF THE EVENTUAL
DEATH OF
EVERY LITERARY
TRADITION.

F. Scott Fitzgerald (1896–1940)

The good writer seems to be writing about himself (but never is) but has his eye always on that thread of the Universe which runs through himself, and all things.

Ralph Waldo Emerson (1803–82)

I've never felt narcissism to be a sin....I think it's necessary to be absolutely in love with ourselves. It's only by reflecting on myself with attention and care that I can reflect on the world. It's only by turning my gaze on myself that I can understand others, feel them as my kin.

Elena Ferrante (unknown)

I approach [writing] as if I'm a priestess. I understand that all the forces are being called upon to help me deliver what is most useful and most nourishing for whoever is reading.

Alice Walker (1944–)

I am fortunate and blessed to be the flute, but I recognize and acknowledge I am not the music.

Sandra Cisneros (1954–)

Why is one compelled to write? To set oneself apart, cocooned, rapt in solitude, despite the wants of others.

Patti Smith (1946–)

I DIDN'T APPLY FOR GRANTS OR WRITERS' CENTERS. I DIDN'T JOIN WRITERS' GROUPS. I JUST COULDN'T DO IT. IT DIDN'T SEEM AN HONEST WAY TO WRITE TO ME. WHEN YOU WRITE ON YOUR OWN, YOU CAN WRITE THE EXTREMES. NO ONE ELSE IS WATCHING AND YOU CAN REALLY GO AS FAR AS YOU NEED TO.

Kiran Desai (1971–)

I've referred to a novel as
a job. But it can also be much
more fantastic than that:
an alternative universe you
enter through concentration
and writing. But of course
it's difficult to set your life
up to accommodate an
alternative universe, which
is why writing one can
take a long time.

Lorrie Moore (1957–)

Surely it is a magical thing for a handful of words, artfully arranged, to stop time. To conjure a place, a person, a situation, in all its specificity and dimensions. To affect us and alter us, as profoundly as real people and things do.

Jhumpa Lahiri (1967–)

I HAVE A LOT OF FAITH
IN WHAT CAN BE ACHIEVED
WITH A WELL-POLISHED
ENGLISH SENTENCE.
NOT THAT I TRY TO
MAKE THE LANGUAGE
OLD-FASHIONED, BUT
I LIKE A CLEAN SENTENCE.

Teju Cole (1975–)

I am not particularly interested in language. Or rather, I am interested in what language can do for me, and I spend many hours each day trying to ensure my prose is as simple as it can possibly be.

Nick Hornby (1957–)

I'M GLAD YOU LIKE ADVERBS— I ADORE THEM.

Henry James (1843–1916)

WHEN YOU CATCH AN ADJECTIVE, KILL IT.

Mark Twain (1835–1910)

If any ideas are to be found in what I write, those ideas came after the writing. I mean, I began by the writing, I began by the story, I began with the dream, if you want to call it that. And then afterwards, perhaps, some idea came of it. But I didn't begin, as I say, by the moral and then writing a fable to prove it.

Jorge Luis Borges (1899–1986)

I write entirely to find out what I'm thinking, what I'm looking at, what I see and what it means. What I want and what I fear....What is going on in these pictures in my mind?

Joan Didion (1934–)

IT'S AMAZING WHAT HAVING AN IDEA FOR A NOVEL WILL FORCE YOU TO DO, AND THE WORLDS THAT YOU WILL ENTER. YOU'LL HAVE TO LEARN TO BE CONVINCING TO PEOPLE WHO KNOW THOSE WORLDS REALLY, REALLY WELL.

Peter Carey (1943–)

I always have these ideas, and I think, "That would be really good; if I was a better writer, I could pull it off." And then I try to become a better writer to do it justice.

Colson Whitehead (1969–)

IF YOU HAVE A THOUGHT,
AN IDEA, A CHANGE, DON'T
EVER DELAY PUTTING
IT DOWN—NOT EVEN FOR
THREE SECONDS.
IT WILL ESCAPE FOREVER.
NO AMOUNT OF PLEADING,
PRAYER, OR CURSING
WILL BRING IT BACK.

Richard Goodman (1945–)

I tried to keep
[a notebook],
but I never could
remember where
I put the damn
thing. I always say
I'm going to keep
one tomorrow.

Dorothy Parker (1893–1967)

To me, writing is entirely mysterious. If I didn't believe it was a mystery, the whole thing wouldn't be worthwhile. I don't know not just how something is going to end but what the next couple of lines are going to be.

William Trevor (1928–2016)

Confusion is the best place to start a story.

Amy Tan (1952–)

The first draft is torture! **It's so hard for me. Once I've written the first draft, I have the pieces to the puzzle, and I love to put it together and make it into a whole.**

Judy Blume (1938–)

The restless condition in which I wander up and down my room with the first page of my new book before me defies all description. I feel as if nothing would do me the least good but setting up a Balloon. It might be inflated in the garden in front—but I am afraid of its scarcely clearing those little houses.

Charles Dickens (1812–70)

BEFORE I START A BOOK I'VE USUALLY GOT FOUR HUNDRED PAGES OF NOTES. MOST OF THEM ARE ALMOST INCOHERENT. BUT THERE'S ALWAYS A MOMENT WHEN YOU FEEL YOU'VE GOT A NOVEL STARTED. YOU CAN MORE OR LESS SEE HOW IT'S GOING TO WORK OUT. AFTER THAT IT'S JUST A QUESTION OF DETAIL.

P. G. Wodehouse (1881–1975)

WRITING A NOVEL IS AS IF
YOU ARE GOING OFF ON A JOURNEY
ACROSS A VALLEY. THE VALLEY
IS FULL OF MIST, BUT YOU CAN SEE
THE TOP OF A TREE HERE AND
THE TOP OF ANOTHER TREE OVER
THERE. AND WITH ANY LUCK
YOU CAN SEE THE OTHER SIDE
OF THE VALLEY. BUT YOU CANNOT
SEE DOWN INTO THE MIST.
NEVERTHELESS, YOU HEAD FOR
THE FIRST TREE.

Terry Pratchett (1948–2015)

A piece of writing has to start somewhere, go somewhere, and sit down when it gets there. You do that by building what you hope is an unarguable structure. Beginning, middle, end.

John McPhee (1931–)

When structure is done well, it should be like architecture: **you sense the overall feel of the building—tall, or airy, or strong—but you're not looking at the buttresses that hold it up or the seams where parts are fastened together.**

Celeste Ng (1980–)

I conceive my subjects like a man—that is, rather more architectonically and dramatically than most women—and then execute them like a woman; or rather, I sacrifice, to my desire for construction and breadth, the small incidental effects that women have always excelled in, the episodical characterization, I mean.

Edith Wharton (1862–1937)

It's the small, unlovely places of life that have always called most eloquently to me: they're the ones that traditional histories tend to overlook, but they often provide the settings for some of our most intense personal dramas—especially, perhaps, if we are women.

Sarah Waters (1966–)

Men write dark stories all the time, and rarely is that darkness obsessed over. But when women write dark, all of a sudden it's a thing. It's like: Why so dark?

Roxane Gay (1974–)

IF YOU CAN MAKE
A PIECE OF WRITING
FUNNY, YOU CAN GET
AWAY WITH ALMOST
ANYTHING—YOU
CAN GET VERY DARK,
YOU CAN MOCK THE
VERY POWERFUL,
AND YOU CAN TRICK
PEOPLE INTO EAGERLY
CONSUMING IDEAS
THAT ARE NORMALLY
VERY THREATENING.

Lindy West (1982–)

I HAVE NEVER FULLY EXORCISED SHAMES THAT STRUCK ME TO THE HEART AS A CHILD EXCEPT THROUGH WRITTEN VIOLENCE, SHADOWY CARICATURE, AND DARK JOKES.

Louise Erdrich (1954–)

Perhaps writing in general is shame management. Certainly female writing has to radically address this problem.

Anne Enright (1962–)

The thought of a married woman writing a story about a marriage gives me a kind of queasy, embarrassed feeling. What a clichéd waste of time! And therein lies the challenge: this shame.

Miranda July (1974–)

ALL LITERATURE IS ABOUT LOVE. WHEN MEN DO IT, IT'S A POLITICAL COMMENT ON HUMAN RELATIONS. WHEN WOMEN DO IT, IT'S JUST A LOVE STORY.

Chimamanda Ngozi Adichie (1977–)

I write about love because it's the most important thing in the world. I write about sex because often it feels like the most important thing in the world. But I set these personal private passions against an outside world— sometimes hostile, usually strange—so that we can see what happens when inner and outer realities collide.

Jeanette Winterson (1959–)

My heroines are always virgins. They never go to bed without a ring on their fingers— not until page 118 at least.

Barbara Cartland (1901–2000)

I try to keep deep love out
of my stories because, once
that particular subject comes
up, it is almost impossible
to talk about anything else.
Readers don't want to hear
about anything else. They go
gaga about love. If a lover
in a story wins his true love,
that's the end of the tale, even
if World War III is about to
begin, and the sky is black
with flying saucers.

Kurt Vonnegut (1922–2007)

Love, like death, is congenial to a novelist because it ends a book conveniently.

E. M. Forster (1879–1970)

I HAVE A COLD
ATTITUDE TO MY
CHARACTERS.
AND I DON'T
PREPARE READERS
FOR SOMETHING
TERRIBLE. I JUST
BRING IT OUT.
I PREFER SHOCK
TREATMENT.

Muriel Spark (1918–2006)

I have this tremendous urge to push the characters off a cliff, which I have to hold back from.

Alan Hollinghurst (1954–)

*I suppose you could say
there is an element of the
laboratory about all fiction
writing. To some extent
they're thought experiments....
There is that slightly chilly
aspect to writing fiction—
you do have to be slightly
detached to say: How would
human beings respond in
this situation?*

Kazuo Ishiguro (1954–)

There is a splinter of ice in the heart of a writer.

Graham Greene (1904–1991)

YOU MUST BE ABLE TO SUMMON EMPATHY FOR ALL YOUR CHARACTERS, EVEN AND ESPECIALLY THE DESPICABLE ONES.

Hanya Yanagihara (1974–)

I have a fondness for
all of my characters,
even the bad guys who
are bad because they
are selfish or dumb or
lazy. I only had one
really evil guy, I thought,
and I didn't care much
for him…his mother was
nice to him, you know,
but he wasn't nice to
his mother.

Elmore Leonard (1925–2013)

People act out of selfishness and a desire to avoid pain, but sometimes they act in ways that are mysterious to themselves....Terrible things happen and nobody learns anything. I wanted to move away from notions of what a character has to earn or realize, and aim for some kind of truth that has more to do with life as I know it.

Emma Cline (1989–)

THERE'S SOMETHING DISHONEST ABOUT BEING KIND TO MY CHARACTERS, BECAUSE THE WORLD, SO OFTEN, ISN'T KIND TO THEM. I THOUGHT ABOUT THAT WITH ALL MY CHARACTERS. IT WAS CONSTANTLY ON MY MIND. I HAD TO BE HONEST. I HAD TO BE RUTHLESS.

Jesmyn Ward (1977–)

The story doesn't want to be told what to do. You have to enter into this process with a high level of trust that the many hours of choosing that you're doing every day will gradually clarify the narrative for you.

George Saunders (1958–)

MY CHAR- ACTERS ARE GALLEY SLAVES.

Vladimir Nabokov (1899–1977)

The legacy of the fairy story in my brain is that everything will work out. In fiction it would be very hard for me, as a writer, to give a bad ending to a good character, or give a good ending to a bad character.

Kate Atkinson (1951–)

THE STORY OR THE CHARACTERS HAVE A LIFE OF THEIR OWN. I CAN'T CONTROL THEM. I WANT THE CHARACTERS TO BE HAPPY, TO GET MARRIED, AND TO HAVE A LOT OF CHILDREN AND LIVE HAPPILY EVER AFTER, BUT IT NEVER HAPPENS THAT WAY.

Isabel Allende (1942–)

To write, I like a room with a view, preferably a long view. I dislike looking out on gardens. I prefer looking at the sea, or ships, or anything that has a vista to it. Oddly enough, I've never worked in the mountains.

Norman Mailer (1923–2007)

Appealing workplaces are
to be avoided. One wants
a room with no view,
so imagination can meet
memory in the dark.

Annie Dillard (1945–)

Don't write in public places.... It should be done only in private, like any other lavatorial activity.

Geoff Dyer (1958–)

In a newspaper office, you realize you don't need to be in a quiet room to write. You have to write in a park or a pub or in a telephone box to get out of the rain. You short-circuit those sensitivities that writers develop. Proust would have saved money on his cork-lined bedroom had he worked for a while at *Le Figaro*.

Michael Frayn (1933–)

I STARTED DRINKING SHORTLY AFTER I STARTED WRITING. AND THEN I KIND OF GOT IT IN MY HEAD THAT I NEEDED TO BE DRINKING WHILE I WROTE....I DON'T KNOW WHY I WAS SO CONVINCED OF IT— IT'S LIKE SAYING "I CAN'T SING UNLESS I HAVE A BLUE SHIRT ON."

David Sedaris (1956–)

I work from 10:30 am
to mid-afternoon,
not stopping for lunch.
I drink lots of coffee
and smoke cigarettes.
Smoking is so tied
to writing I could
not give it up.

Martin Amis (1949–)

I FOUND THAT THREE HOURS
A DAY IS ABOUT ALL I CAN DO OF
ACTUAL COMPOSING. I COULD
DO POLISHING PERHAPS LATER.
I SOMETIMES FOUND AT FIRST
THAT I WANTED TO GO ON LONGER,
BUT WHEN I LOOKED AT THE STUFF
THE NEXT DAY, WHAT I'D DONE
AFTER THE THREE HOURS WERE
UP WAS NEVER SATISFACTORY.
IT'S MUCH BETTER TO STOP AND
THINK ABOUT SOMETHING ELSE
QUITE DIFFERENT.

T. S. Eliot (1888–1965)

Two thousand words is a good day's work.

Evelyn Waugh (1903–66)

THE WRITER SAYS

How to write: *butt in chair.* Start each day anywhere. Let yourself do it badly. Just take one passage at a time. Get butt back in chair.

Anne Lamott (1954–)

112

I… venture to advise young men who look forward to authorship as the business of their lives… to avoid enthusiastic rushes with their pens, and to seat themselves at their desks day by day as though they were lawyers' clerks—and so let them sit until the allotted task shall be accomplished.

Anthony Trollope (1815–82)

BE A GOOD STEWARD OF YOUR GIFTS. PROTECT YOUR TIME. FEED YOUR INNER LIFE. AVOID TOO MUCH NOISE. READ GOOD BOOKS, HAVE GOOD SENTENCES IN YOUR EARS. BE BY YOURSELF AS OFTEN AS YOU CAN. WALK. TAKE THE PHONE OFF THE HOOK. WORK REGULAR HOURS.

Jane Kenyon (1947–95)

Get a dog....
Being a dog owner requires a similar form of discipline [to writing]. You wake up every morning. You walk the dog. You do this whether you're tired, depressed, broke, hung over, or have been recently dumped. You do it.

Jennifer Weiner (1970–)

Here's a short list of what not to do when you sit down to write. Don't answer the phone. Don't look at e-mail. Don't go on the Internet for any reason.

Dani Shapiro (1962–)

DON'T HAVE CHILDREN.

Richard Ford (1944–)

It wasn't the housework or the children that dragged me down. I'd done housework all my life. It was the sort of open rule that women who tried to do anything so weird as writing were unseemly and possibly neglectful.

Alice Munro (1931–)

Composition seems to me Impossible, with a head full of Joints of Mutton and doses of rhubarb.

Jane Austen (1775–1817)

YOU CAN ONLY WRITE REGULARLY IF YOU'RE WILLING TO WRITE BADLY. YOU CAN'T WRITE REGULARLY AND WELL. ONE SHOULD ACCEPT BAD WRITING AS A WAY OF PRIMING THE PUMP, A WARM-UP EXERCISE THAT ALLOWS YOU TO WRITE WELL.

Jennifer Egan (1962–)

You can always fix bad pages. You can't fix no pages.

Harlan Coben (1962–)

I do not rework poems, but let them go at first sitting, because if I have lied originally, there's no use driving the spikes home, and if I haven't lied, well hell, there's nothing to worry about.

Charles Bukowski (1920–94)

I REALLY ENJOY REVISING MORE THAN WRITING. I LOVE TO CROSS THINGS OUT AND CUT A PAGE DOWN TO ONE PARAGRAPH.

Beverly Cleary (1916–)

For me [writing is] mostly a question of rewriting.

James Thurber (1894–1961)

THERE'S A POINT
AT WHICH YOU'RE
NOT MAKING IT
BETTER; YOU'RE
JUST MAKING IT
DIFFERENT. YOU
HAVE TO BE GOOD
AT RECOGNIZING
THAT POINT.

Salman Rushdie (1947–)

You know when a piece is finished, because you can't pull out a single sentence or change a word or syllable.

Charles Johnson (1948–)

Any piece of writing is just the last proof; it's the one we had to let go of because the deadline is here.

Roger Angell (1920–)

It's never a day job; it's always a tremendous challenge. People always ask me, "Do you ever start a book and then put it aside and do something different?" And, unfortunately, no, I always write everything right to the bitter end.

Edmund White (1940–)

THEY CAN'T YANK [A] NOVELIST LIKE THEY CAN [A] PITCHER. [A] NOVELIST HAS TO GO THE FULL NINE, EVEN IF IT KILLS HIM.

Ernest Hemingway (1899–1961)

YOU ARE ABSOLUTELY A BEGINNER— EVERY DAY. YOU HAVE NO RIGHT TO ASSUME THAT YOU'LL BE ABLE TO WRITE BECAUSE YOU COULD WRITE YESTERDAY.

Hilary Mantel (1952–)

The scary thing about writing novels is that they're all different. What worked last time, won't this time, and there's always that little voice that whispers to you that this time you've bitten off more than you can chew, located the very story that will show you who's boss (not you).

Richard Russo (1949–)

I DON'T HAVE ANY ANXIETY ABOUT WRITING. NOT REALLY. IT'S SUCH A PLEASURE, AND OUR LIVES ARE SO RELATIVELY EASY COMPARED TO PEOPLE WHO ARE REALLY OUT THERE IN THE WORLD WORKING HARD AND SUFFERING.

Joyce Carol Oates (1938–)

Anyone who
writes or chooses
a writing life
is walking off
the edge of the
universe into
the big dark
naked and crying.

Lidia Yuknavitch (1963–)

Every time I read that someone has spoken badly of me I begin to cry, I drag myself across the floor, I scratch myself, I stop writing indefinitely, I lose my appetite, I smoke less, I engage in sport, I go for walks on the edge of the sea, which by the way is less than thirty meters from my house, and I ask the seagulls, whose ancestors ate the fish who ate Ulysses: Why me? Why? I've done you no harm.

Roberto Bolaño (1953–2003)

WHEN GOD HANDS YOU A GIFT, HE ALSO HANDS YOU A WHIP; AND THE WHIP IS INTENDED SOLELY FOR SELF-FLAGELLATION.

Truman Capote (1924–84)

The effort of writing seems more arduous all the time. Unlike technicians who are supposed to become more proficient with practice, I find I've grown considerably less articulate.

S. J. Perelman (1904–79)

ALL WRITERS FEEL STRUCK BY THE LIMITATIONS OF LANGUAGE.

Margaret Atwood (1939–)

In the end a man must sit down and get the words on paper, and against great odds. This takes stamina and resolution.

E. B. White (1899–1985)

No writer who achieves spectacular success does so without a modicum of good luck.

P. D. James (1920–2014)

[The] impulse—to tell a tale rich in context, alive to situation, shot through with event and perspective—is as strong in human beings as the need to eat food and breathe air: it may be suppressed but it can never be destroyed.

Vivian Gornick (1935–)

A WRITER IS A
WRITER BECAUSE
EVEN WHEN
THERE IS NO
HOPE, EVEN
WHEN NOTHING
YOU DO SHOWS
ANY SIGN OF
PROMISE, YOU
KEEP WRITING
ANYWAY.

Junot Díaz (1968–)

I'm always thinking about duties, rights, and gifts.... That's how social worlds and our intimate lives are structured, right? What is your duty? What accrues to you? What is your right? And what are your gifts? The wildcard is gifts because what rights accrue to you because of certain gifts?

Zadie Smith (1975–)

There's no moral obligation to write in any particular way. But there is a moral obligation, I think, not to ally yourself with power against the powerless.

Chinua Achebe (1930–2013)

I'm not a big believer in the novelist's obligation to reflect or catalyze society in some ways.... I don't write books that have messages. None of them have a moral to them. I'm more interested in exploring things that are hard to understand and maybe bringing the readers with me.

Tana French (1973–)

What a novel can do is show the distance between what's being said and what's being felt....The drama is the distance between what's to be spoken of and what's not to be mentioned again.

Colm Tóibín (1955–)

If being a novelist has any moral, political side, it is identifying with people who are not like you. It's not that we make political statements or show our party cards; it's seeing the world through the eyes of someone who is different.

Orhan Pamuk (1952–)

LITERATURE IS POWERLESS IN DIRECTLY CONFRONTING THE EVIL, BUT IT CAN BE SUBVERSIVE AND EFFECTIVE IN SHAPING READERS' SENSIBILITIES AND CHANGING THEIR WAY OF SEEING THINGS. IT IS A SLOW PROCESS.

Ha Jin (1956–)

CREATE DANGEROUSLY,
FOR PEOPLE WHO
READ DANGEROUSLY.
THIS IS WHAT I'VE ALWAYS
THOUGHT IT MEANT
TO BE A WRITER. WRITING,
KNOWING IN PART
THAT NO MATTER HOW
TRIVIAL YOUR WORDS
MAY SEEM, SOMEDAY,
SOMEWHERE, SOMEONE
MAY RISK HIS OR
HER LIFE TO READ THEM.

Edwidge Danticat (1969–)

Writers throughout the ages
have one weapon, which is
literature, but they also have
their responsibilities as
a citizen when literature does
not seem to suffice....They
are not mutually exclusive.
One continues to write
anyway, but if you are called
out to demonstrate, if people
are being killed in the streets,
it's hardly the moment to
go for your pen and paper.

Wole Soyinka (1934–)

READING IS AN ACTIVE, IMAGINATIVE ACT; IT TAKES WORK.

Khaled Hosseini (1965–)

The demand that I make of my reader is that he should devote his whole life to reading my works.

James Joyce (1882–1941)

Whether I'm writing scripts or prose, the goal is identical. To give pleasure. Now whether I succeed or not is up for debate, and, mostly, I fail. But I try. I like to make things. It's a way to stay busy during one's ephemeral and confusing life.

Jonathan Ames (1964–)

On my tombstone, I want to have the words "She gave a lot of people a lot of pleasure."

Jackie Collins (1937–2015)

THE REAL TROUBLE WITH THE WRITING GAME IS THAT NO GENERAL RULE CAN BE WORKED OUT FOR UNIFORM GUIDANCE.

Erle Stanley Gardner (1889–1970)

You write what you write, and then either it holds up or it doesn't hold up. There are no rules.

Jamaica Kincaid (1949–)

Achebe, Chinua 143
Adichie, Chimamanda Ngozi 87
Alexie, Sherman 19
Allende, Isabel 103
Ames, Jonathan 152
Amis, Kingsley 15
Amis, Martin 109
Angell, Roger 127
Atkinson, Kate 102
Atwood, Margaret 137
Austen, Jane 119
Baldwin, James 44
Bass, Rick 160
Blume, Judy 74
Bolaño, Roberto 134
Borges, Jorge Luis 66
Boyd, William 41
Boylan, Jennifer Finney 29
Bradbury, Ray 51
Bukowski, Charles 122
Butler, Octavia 17
Capote, Truman 135
Carey, Peter 68
Cartland, Barbara 89
Chandler, Raymond 35
Cisneros, Sandra 57
Cleary, Beverly 123
Cline, Emma 98
Coates, Ta-Nehisi 7
Coben, Harlan 121
Cole, Teju 62
Collins, Jackie 153
Danticat, Edwidge 148
Desai, Kiran 59
Díaz, Junot 141
Dickens, Charles 75
Didion, Joan 67
Dillard, Annie 105

Dyer, Geoff 106
Egan, Jennifer 120
Eggers, Dave 26
Eliot, T. S. 110
Emerson, Ralph Waldo 54
Enright, Anne 85
Erdrich, Louise 84
Ferrante, Elena 55
Fitzgerald, F. Scott 53
Fleming, Ian 40
Ford, Richard 117
Forster, E. M. 91
Frayn, Michael 107
French, Tana 144
Gaitskill, Mary 28
García Márquez, Gabriel 43
Gardam, Jane 25
Gardner, Erle Stanley 154
Gay, Roxane 82
Gilchrist, Ellen 30
Goodman, Richard 70
Gornick, Vivian 140
Greene, Graham 95
Grossman, David 9
Hammett, Dashiell 24
Hemingway, Ernest 129
Hinton, S. E. 18
Hollinghurst, Alan 93
hooks, bell 45
Hornby, Nick 63
Hosseini, Khaled 150
Hurston, Zora Neale 31
Ishiguro, Kazuo 94
James, Henry 64
James, Marlon 52
James, P. D. 139
Jin, Ha 147
Johnson, Charles 126

Joyce, James 151
July, Miranda 86
Kazin, Alfred 11
Kenyon, Jane 114
Kincaid, Jamaica 155
King, Stephen 8
Kirino, Natsuo 39
Klinkenborg, Verlyn 12
Koch, Herman 33
Kraus, Chris 27
Kureishi, Hanif 16
Lahiri, Jhumpa 61
Lamott, Anne 112
le Carré, John 14
Lee, Chang-Rae 46
Lee, Min Jin 36
Leonard, Elmore 97
Mailer, Norman 104
Mantel, Hilary 130
Marías, Javier 20
Maxwell, William 13
McPhee, John 78
Moore, Lorrie 60
Morrison, Toni 21
Munro, Alice 118
Murakami, Haruki 42
Nabokov, Vladimir 101
Ng, Celeste 79
Oates, Joyce Carol 132
Pamuk, Orhan 146
Parker, Dorothy 71
Perelman, S. J. 136
Picoult, Jodi 50
Pratchett, Terry 77
Rowling, J. K. 32
Rushdie, Salman 125
Russo, Richard 131
Saunders, George 100

Sedaris, David 108
Seth, Vikram 22
Shapiro, Dani 116
Shteyngart, Gary 34
Smith, Patti 58
Smith, Zadie 142
Soyinka, Wole 149
Spark, Muriel 92
Straub, Emma 37
Straub, Peter 47
Tan, Amy 73
Theroux, Paul 23
Thurber, James 124
Tóibín, Colm 145
Trevor, William 72
Trollope, Anthony 113
Twain, Mark 65
VanderMeer, Jeff 49
Vonnegut, Kurt 90
Walker, Alice 56
Ward, Jesmyn 99
Waters, Sarah 81
Waugh, Evelyn 111
Weiner, Jennifer 115
Welty, Eudora 48
West, Lindy 83
Wharton, Edith 80
White, E. B. 138
White, Edmund 128
Whitehead, Colson 69
Winterson, Jeanette 88
Wodehouse, P. G. 76
Woolf, Virginia 10
Yanagihara, Hanya 96
Yuknavitch, Lidia 133
Zinsser, William 38

Published by
Princeton Architectural Press
A McEvoy Group company
202 Warren Street
Hudson, NY 12534
Visit our website at www.papress.com

Printed in China
21 20 19 18 4 3 2 1 First edition

ISBN: 978-1-61689-721-5

Princeton Architectural Press is
a leading publisher in architecture,
design, photography, landscape,
and visual culture. We create fine books
and stationery of unsurpassed quality
and production values. With more
than one thousand titles published,
we find design everywhere and in the
most unlikely places.

Editor: Sara Stemen
Designer: Brett Yasko
Series designer: Paul Wagner

Special thanks to:
Janet Behning, Abby Bussel,
Benjamin English, Jan Cigliano
Hartman, Susan Hershberg,
Kristen Hewitt, Lia Hunt,
Valerie Kamen, Jennifer Lippert,
Sara McKay, Parker Menzimer,
Eliana Miller, Nina Pick, Wes Seeley,
Rob Shaeffer, Marisa Tesoro,
and Joseph Weston of Princeton
Architectural Press
—Kevin C. Lippert, publisher

Library of Congress
Cataloging-in-Publication Data
is available from the publisher
upon request.

Write every day. Don't ever stop.

Rick Bass (1958–)